W9-AUD-503

Rock It!™

WEATHERING AND EROSION
WEARING DOWN ROCKS

Steven M. Hoffman

PowerKiDS press

New York

Published in 2011 by The Rosen Publishing Group, Inc.
29 East 21st Street, New York, NY 10010

First Edition

Editor: Amelie von Zumbusch
Book Design: Kate Laczynski
Layout Design: Ashley Burrell

Photo Credits: Cover, pp. 4, 14, 18 Shutterstock.com; p. 6 © www.iStockphoto.com/Chris Pritchard; p. 8 © www.iStockphoto.com/Frank Moroni; p. 10 Harald Sund/Getty Images; p. 12 Photography by Mangiwau/Getty Images; p. 16 © www.iStockphoto.com/desertsolitaire; p. 20 Martin Page/Getty Images.

Library of Congress Cataloging-in-Publication Data

Hoffman, Steven M. (Steven Michael), 1960-
  Weathering and erosion : wearing down rocks / by Steven M. Hoffman. — 1st ed.
     p. cm. — (Rock it!)
  Includes index.
  ISBN 978-1-4488-2710-7 (library binding) — ISBN 978-1-4488-2711-4 (pbk.) —
  ISBN 978-1-4488-2712-1 (6-pack)
  1. Weathering—Juvenile literature. 2. Erosion—Juvenile literature. I. Title.
  QE570.H64 2011
  551.3'02—dc22
                                    2010032777

Manufactured in the United States of America

CPSIA Compliance Information: Batch #WW11PK: For Further Information contact Rosen Publishing, New York, New York at 1-800-237-9932

CONTENTS

This is the Fish River Canyon, in Namibia. The canyon is about 100 miles (161 km) long. It is the result of weathering and erosion.

Changing Land

A heavy rain fell on a mountain. Water flowed down its slopes and ran into a stream. The water was dark with **silt** and sand. It picked up this **sediment** as it flowed over the ground. The stream carried away a little bit of the mountain that day.

Land seems never to change. However, it does change very slowly over time. Water, ice, and wind break apart rock and carry it away. The breaking apart of rock is called weathering. The picking up and carrying away of the pieces is erosion. Over a long time, weathering and erosion can wear down mountains, fill in valleys, and cut deep **canyons**.

These caves were formed out of limestone by chemical weathering. Limestone is one of the stones most often worn away by chemical weathering.

Water and Air

Weathering occurs in many ways. **Chemical weathering** happens when the **minerals** and other matter from which rocks are made change. This kind of weathering almost always occurs with water.

There are several types of chemical weathering. The simplest kind is when rock just **dissolves** in water. Other kinds of chemical weathering happen when gases mix into water. When the gas carbon dioxide mixes into water, the water acts like a weak **acid**. This acidic water is very good at breaking down rocks. Oxygen gas also mixes into water. This makes some rocks rust. The rocks become weakened and break apart easily.

This big rock has been split in half by physical weathering. All rocks, big or small, can be broken down by weathering.

Breaking Rock

Chemical weathering breaks down the minerals and other matter in rock. Other kinds of weathering just break rock into smaller pieces. These types of weathering are called **physical weathering**.

Physical weathering can occur when the Sun's heat makes rocks hot. A cool rain might then fall on the rocks and cool them down. This quick change makes the rocks crack a little bit. Pieces soon fall off onto the ground.

Ice also breaks apart rock. Water can seep into cracks in rocks. As the water freezes to ice, it expands, pushing open the cracks. In time, the rocks break apart.

Rock that is buried in Earth has a lot of heavy rock pressing down on it. When the rock above it wears away, the deeply buried rock can crack into sheets.

Here, you can see how tree roots surround a rock and work their way into the rock's cracks. This is an important cause of weathering.

Plants and Animals

Plants can also cause weathering. Plant roots grow into cracks in rock to get water. The growing roots slowly push open the cracks. The cracked rock then breaks apart easily.

Plant roots also give off acids. The acids break down rock as the roots push it apart.

Animals can break apart rock, too. For example, prairie dogs and groundhogs dig tunnels in soft rock. The animals break the rock into many small pieces. They also move pieces of rock around. This lets water get to the rock. The pieces of rock break down faster than a solid layer of rock would.

In this photo, you can see the sediment that this river is carrying. You can also see where the sediment was dropped as the river flows into the sea.

Washed Away

After weathering breaks rock apart, erosion picks up the pieces and moves them away. Of all the ways that erosion occurs, movement by water is the most important.

Water erosion begins as rain falls on land. This water carries silt and sand downhill to streams. Silt stays in the water, making it look dirty. Sand and bigger pieces of rock skip or roll along the stream's bottom. Streams carry the sediment until the water slows. Then, it is dropped on a sandbar or **delta**.

Some streams cut down through rock as they flow along. Fast-flowing water erodes deeper and deeper until it cuts a canyon into the rock.

This huge sheet of ice is the Mendenhall Glacier.
It is near Juneau, Alaska. The glacier has helped
shape the land around it.

14

A Flow of Ice

Glaciers are a powerful cause of erosion. A glacier is a large mass of ice that forms from snow. Glacial ice flows slowly under its own weight.

Glaciers cause erosion by scratching and digging the rock below. Rocks held in glacial ice scratch the rock beneath the glacier. Glaciers also pick up loose soil and broken rock. This digging can make deep holes that later become lakes.

As a glacier moves along, wet sediment may freeze to its bottom. This forms a layer of dirty ice at the bottom of the glacier. When the ice melts, sediment gets left behind.

Much of the northern United States is covered by sediment that melted out of glaciers. This kind of sediment is called till.

This cloud of dust is part of a big dust storm in Arizona. Dust storms can be very unsafe. It is hard for people and animals to see or breathe during them.

Blowing in the Wind

Wind causes erosion by picking up and moving small grains of silt and sand. In many places, plants hold soil in place. However, in dry places that have few plants, dust storms occur. Winds blow low, dark clouds of fine sediment across the land. When the wind slows, the sediment falls to the ground.

In sandy deserts, the wind picks up sand. The heavy sand grains skip along the ground. The sand piles up into **dunes** in some places. The dunes move slowly as sand blows up one side and falls down the other.

The sand falling down some sand dunes makes a sound. This sound can be like a slow booming or a song. Such dunes are called singing sand dunes.

Delicate Arch, seen here, is the best-known arch in Arches National Park. It was formed by the weathering and erosion of sandstone rock.

Canyons and Arches

Weathering and erosion have formed many beautiful places. The Grand Canyon, in Arizona, has colorful rock walls and is about 1 mile (2 km) deep. The canyon was cut into the rock by the Colorado River over millions of years. The river still flows at the bottom. It continues to make the canyon deeper.

Arches National Park, in Utah, has large rock arches. The arches formed as weathering and erosion widened cracks in the rock. After a lot of time had passed, wall-like sheets of rock remained. These walls of rock then eroded in the middle, leaving beautiful arches of yellow, orange, and red rock.

The coast at Birling Gap, in East Essex, England, is eroding. The homes along this coast are in danger of falling into the sea!

Erosion Problems

Erosion sometimes causes problems. Flooding mountain streams can move stones as big as cars. The stones and smaller rocks might make bridges fall down. Heavy rains in mountains can cause **mudflows**. A mudflow is a flow of water and sediment. Mudflows can move down mountainsides quickly. They may cover roads or train tracks.

Glaciers sometimes advance quickly, as much as 10 yards (9 m) each day. The moving ice can dam rivers and cause floods.

Wind erosion also causes problems. Large sand dunes can move onto farms and bury houses. People try to stop the dunes by building **windbreaks** and growing plants on top of the sand.

Signs of Change

Weathering and erosion occur everywhere. You can see weathering in places where plants grow through the sidewalk. They push apart the stone or concrete and break it into pieces.

The signs of erosion are easy to see on bare hills. You can see small cuts of bare earth in the hillside and sediment piled up at its bottom.

When you travel, near your home or far away, watch for signs of weathering and erosion. Think about how weathering and erosion shaped and are still shaping the places you see. You will enjoy stream valleys, canyons, and beautiful arches in a special way.

GLOSSARY

acid (A-sud) A thing that breaks down matter faster than water does.

arches (AHRCH-ez) Things that have sides that curve over an open space in the middle.

canyons (KAN-yunz) Deep, narrow valleys.

chemical weathering (KEH-mih-kul WEH-ther-ing) The breaking down of rocks by changing the matter of which they are made.

delta (DEL-tuh) A pile of earth and sand that collects at the mouth of a river.

dissolves (dih-ZOLVZ) Breaks down.

dunes (DOONZ) Hills of sand piled up by the wind.

glaciers (GLAY-shurz) Large masses of ice that move down mountains or along valleys.

minerals (MIN-rulz) Natural matter that is not an animal, a plant, or another living thing.

mudflows (MUD-flohz) Heavy flows of mud and dirt.

physical weathering (FIH-zih-kul WEH-ther-ing) The breaking down of rocks into smaller pieces.

sediment (SEH-deh-ment) Gravel, sand, or mud carried by wind or water.

silt (SILT) Fine bits of earth, smaller than sand grains.

windbreaks (WIND-brayks) Things built to block the wind and things blown by the wind.

INDEX

WEB SITES

Due to the changing nature of Internet links, PowerKids Press has developed an online list of Web sites related to the subject of this book. This site is updated regularly. Please use this link to access the list:
www.powerkidslinks.com/rockit/weather/